The Crafter's Design Library

Animals

Sharon Bennett

D&C
David and Charles

Wiv luv 'n' stuff to Andrew John x

A DAVID & CHARLES BOOK
Copyright © David & Charles Limited 2006

David & Charles is an F+W Publications Inc. company
4700 East Galbraith Road
Cincinnati, OH 45236

First published in the UK in 2006
First US paperback edition 2006

Text and illustrations copyright © Sharon Bennett 2006

A catalogue record for this book is available from the British Library.

ISBN-13: 978-0-7153-2473-8 hardback
ISBN-10: 0-7153-2473-X hardback

ISBN-13: 978-0-7153-2474-5 paperback
ISBN-10: 0-7153-2474-8 paperback

Printed in China by RR Donnelley
for David & Charles
Brunel House   Newton Abbot   Devon

Commissioning Editor Jennifer Fox-Proverbs
Assistant Editor Louise Clark
Project Editor Betsy Hosegood
Senior Designer Charly Bailey
Design Assistant Eleanor Stafford
Production Controller Kelly Smith

Visit our website at www.davidandcharles.co.uk

**David & Charles books are available from all good bookshops; alternatively you
can contact our Orderline on 0870 9908222 or write to us at FREEPOST EX2 110,
D&C Direct, Newton Abbot, TQ12 4ZZ (no stamp required UK only); US customers
call 800-289-0963 and Canadian customers call 800-840-5220.**

contents

the essential techniques

the templates

Animal magic

Man's fascination with animal motifs dates back to earliest times, when animals were painted on cave walls. We can't be certain of the significance of these motifs, but it is thought that they were painted to bring luck in the hunt. Certainly they were not purely decorative because some of the motifs are painted at the ends of long, narrow passages and in barely reachable corners of small caves where they would not be easily visible.

Today we are attracted to animal motifs for many reasons. Those of us with pets can take special pleasure in depictions of our treasured animals, while others are simply drawn to particular creatures, such as pigs, frogs, butterflies or fish, for example, without necessarily knowing why. Perhaps it is an animal's perceived character that attracts us, or its associations with qualities such as freedom or love. Whatever the appeal, it's nice to keep the main attractions of each animal in mind while re-creating it in paint, allowing it to inspire and raise the spirits.

So which animals do you want to depict? With more than 350 designs in this book there's something to please everyone. And because there are so many designs to choose from, they've been divided into sections to help you find what you are looking for, whether it's a pet, a safari animal or a fantasy creature. Some designs are aimed specifically at children and those who like the cute and cuddly. Others suit different styles, but every animal is adorable in its own way.

All the motifs are depicted as simple black and white outline drawings, which are easy to photocopy or scan into your computer. If you are new to paper crafting, look at the designs at the start of each chapter first, which are usually the simplest motifs and therefore the easiest to use. However, remember that you can simplify any of the motifs as required, or add embellishments suitable for your particular design.

Whether you are new to crafting or more experienced, make sure you take a look at the first section of the book, which provides information on using the templates and provides some wonderful finished projects to inspire you. In addition to ideas for card making, you'll find suggestions for translating the motifs onto other objects, such as a decorative bird box, a jug, some funky Wellington boots and a peg rail. So think laterally, think creatively and above all allow the templates and the animals depicted to inspire you to try something new.

The designs shown here can be found in the templates section of this book. They are all versatile designs that could be used for a host of applications. See the Project Gallery, pages 20–25 for further inspiration and advice.

Applying motifs to craft media

The techniques best suited to applying your selected motif to a particular medium depend on the surface you are working with. The following pages offer some simple advice on how to do this for the most popular craft media. Guidance is also given on how to enlarge or reduce the motif to suit your requirements (below) and how to create a stencil (page 11).

Enlarging and reducing a motif

Here are three ways to change the size of a motif to suit your project: the traditional method using a grid, or the modern alternatives of a photocopier or scanner.

Using a grid

The traditional method of enlargement involves using a grid. To begin, use low-tack masking tape to secure tracing paper over the original design. Draw a square or rectangle onto the tracing paper, enclosing the image (see below). Use a ruler to divide up the square or rectangle into rows of equally spaced vertical and horizontal lines. Complex designs should have lines about 1cm (³⁄₈in) apart; simpler ones can have lines 4cm (1½in) apart.

Now draw a square or rectangle to match your required design size, and draw a grid to correspond with the one you have just drawn over the image, as shown below. You can now begin to re-create the original image by redrawing it, square by square, at the required scale.

Using a photocopier

For fast and accurate results, use a photocopier to enlarge or reduce a motif. To do this, you need to calculate your enlargement percentage. First measure the width of the image you want to end up with. Here, the motif needs to be enlarged to 120mm (4¾in). Measure the width of the original motif, which in this case is 80mm (3¼in). Divide the first measurement by the second to find the percentage by which you need to enlarge the motif, in this instance 150%. (An enlargement must always be more than 100% and a reduction less than 100%).

To photocopy an image onto tracing paper, use tracing paper that is at least 90gsm. When photocopying an image from tracing paper, place the tracing paper onto the glass, and then lay a sheet of white paper on top of it. This will help to produce a sharp copy.

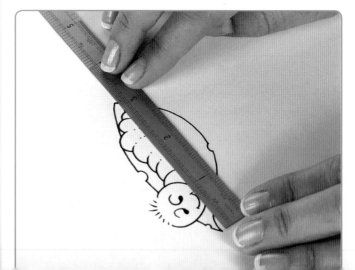

Transferring a motif onto paper, card, wood or fine fabric

A light box makes it easy to trace an image directly onto a piece of paper, thin card or fabric, but if you don't have one it is easy to improvize with household items. Balance a piece of clear plastic across two piles of books or pieces of furniture, and place a table lamp underneath. Place your motif on the plastic and your paper, thin card or fabric on top. Switch on the light and simply trace over the design showing through.

To transfer a design onto wood, thick card or foam, trace the design onto tracing paper using a sharp pencil. Turn the tracing over and redraw on the wrong side with a soft lead pencil. Now turn the tracing over again and use masking tape to secure it right side up onto your chosen surface. Carefully redraw the image (see the photograph below). Press firmly enough to transfer the motif, but take care not to damage the surface.

Using a scanner

A third way to enlarge or reduce a motif is to scan the original image on a flatbed scanner or to photograph it with a digital camera. Once the image is on your computer you can either adjust the size using image manipulation software or simply alter the percentage of your printout size. If the finished result is larger than the printer's capacity, some software will allow you to tile the image over several sheets of paper, which can then be joined together to form the whole image.

An image manipulation package may also allow you to alter the proportions of a motif, making it wider or narrower, for example. Take care not to distort it beyond recognition, though. Once you are happy with your image, it can be saved to be used again and again.

Transferring a motif onto foil

To emboss foil, simply take the original tracing and secure it to the foil surface. Rest the foil on kitchen paper. Use an embossing tool or an old ballpoint pen that has run out of ink to press down on the tracing, embossing the metal below. Use the same technique on the back of the foil to produce a raised effect.

Transferring a motif onto mirror and ceramic

Trace the motif onto tracing paper, then turn the tracing over and redraw on the wrong side using a china-graph pencil. A chinagraph produces a waxy line that adheres well to shiny surfaces such as coloured glass, mirrored glass and ceramic. Chinagraphs are prone to blunt quickly, but it doesn't matter if the lines are thick and heavy at this stage. Use masking tape to secure the tracing right side up onto the surface. Carefully redraw with a sharp pencil to transfer the image.

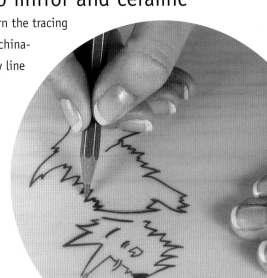

Tracing a motif onto glass and acetate

Roughly cut out the motif and tape it to the underside of the acetate or glass with masking tape. It is helpful to rest glassware on a few sheets of kitchen towel for protection and to stop curved objects from rolling. The image will now show through the clear surface, and you can simply trace along the lines with glass outliner or paint directly onto the surface.

If you want to transfer an image onto opaque glass, or onto a container that is difficult to slip a motif behind, such as a bottle with a narrow neck, follow the instructions on page 7 for transferring a motif onto mirror and ceramic.

Transferring a motif onto curved items

Motifs can be transferred onto rounded items, but will need to be adapted to fit the curves. First trace the motif, redrawing it on the underside (use a chinagraph pencil if the container is ceramic). Make cuts in the template from the edge towards the centre. Lay the motif against the surface so that the cuts slightly overlap or spread open, depending on whether the surface is concave or convex. Tape the motif in place with masking tape and transfer the design by drawing over the lines with a sharp pencil.

Making a template for a straight-sided container

If you wish to apply a continuous motif such as a border to a straight-sided container, make a template of the container first. To do this, slip a piece of tracing paper into a transparent glass container or around an opaque glass or ceramic container. Lay the paper smoothly against the surface and tape in place with masking tape. Mark the position of the upper edge of the container with a pencil. Now mark the position of the overlapping ends of the paper or mark each side of the handle on a mug, cup or jug.

Remove the tracing and join the overlap marks, if you have made these. Measure down from the upper edge and mark the upper limit of the band or border on the template. Cut out the template and slip it into or around the container again to check the fit. Transfer your chosen template onto the tracing paper, then onto the container.

Making a template for a plate

1 Cut a square of tracing paper slightly larger than the diameter of the plate. Make a straight cut from one edge to the centre of the paper then roughly cut out a circle from the centre to help the paper lie flat. Place the paper centrally on the plate or saucer and tape one cut edge across the rim. Smooth the paper around the rim and tape in place, overlapping the cut edges. Mark the position of the overlap on the paper.

2 Turn the plate over and draw around the circumference onto the underside of the tracing paper. Remove the paper, then measure the depth of the plate rim and mark it on the paper by measuring in from the circumference. Join the marks with a curved line.

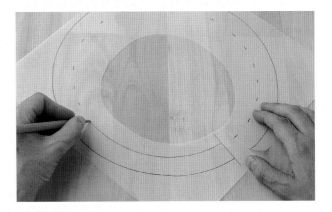

Transferring a motif onto fabric

If fabric is lightweight and pale in colour, it may be possible to trace the motif simply by laying the fabric on top. If the fabric is dark or thick, it may help to use a light box. Place the motif under the fabric on the surface of the light box (see page 7 for information on constructing a home light box). As the light shines up through the motif and fabric you should be able to see the design lines, ready for tracing.

Alternatively, place a piece of dressmaker's carbon paper face down on the fabric and tape the motif on top with masking tape. Trace the design with a sharp pencil to transfer it onto the fabric, as shown below. The marks made by the carbon are easily wiped away.

Transferring a motif onto a knitting chart

Use knitting-chart paper rather than ordinary graph paper to chart a knitting design. (Knitted stitches are wider than they are tall and knitting chart paper is sized accordingly.) Transfer the motif straight onto the knitting graph paper (see page 7 for advice on transferring onto paper). Each square on the graph paper represents a stitch. Make sure that you are happy with the number of squares in the motif, as this dictates the number of stitches in your design, and ultimately the design size. Fill in the applicable squares on the chart using coloured pens or pencils. (The motif shown above is used on page 21.)

Use the finished chart in conjunction with a knitting pattern. Read the chart from right to left for a knit row and from left to right for a purl row. The motif can also be worked on a ready-knitted item with Swiss darning.

Transferring a motif onto needlepoint canvas and cross stitch fabric

Designs on needlepoint canvas and cross stitch fabric can be worked either by referring to the design on a chart, or by transferring the image to the material and stitching over it.

To transfer the motif onto a chart

Transfer the motif straight onto graph paper (see page 7 for advice on transferring onto paper). Each square on the graph paper represents a square of canvas mesh or Aida cross stitch fabric. Colour in the squares that the motif lines cross with coloured pencils or pens. You may want to make half stitches where the motif outline runs through a box. Mark the centre of the design along a vertical and horizontal line (see right) and mark the centre of the fabric lengthways and widthways with tacking stitches.

To transfer the motif directly onto canvas or fabric

With an open-weave canvas or pale fabric it is possible to trace the design directly onto the canvas or fabric. First, mark a small cross centrally on the motif and on the material. On a lightbox (see page 7), place the material on top of the motif,

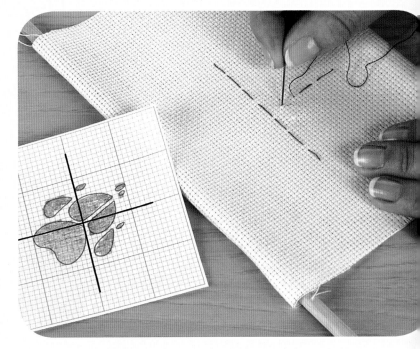

aligning the crosses. Tape in position and trace the image with a waterproof pen. Alternatively, use dressmaker's carbon paper to transfer the design, as explained in transferring a motif onto fabric, opposite.

Making a stencil

Tape a piece of tracing paper over the motif to be adapted into a stencil. Redraw the image, thickening the lines and creating 'bridges' between the sections to be cut out. You may find it helpful to shade in the areas to be cut out. Lay a piece of carbon paper, ink side down, on a stencil sheet, place the tracing on top, right side up, and tape in place. Redraw the design to transfer it to the stencil sheet. Finally, lay the stencil sheet on a cutting mat and carefully cut out the stencil with a craft knife, always drawing the sharp edge of the blade away from you.

Adapting and combining designs

Although you can use the templates in this book exactly as they are, a lot of fun is to be had simply messing around with them, simplifying designs, making them more ornate, combining them and so on. You can do this endlessly, making your library of templates never-ending as your ideas become new images.

Repeating a design

Why use a lovely design once when you can use it repeatedly for greater impact? Here the mosquito from page 84 is rotated and repeated around a central point to create a stunning border.
Do this on a computer by scanning it in first or make a stencil for equally rapid results.

When stencilling on a circular border use a protractor to help with positioning.

Something simple

They say that the simplest things are often the best. Here the tortoise motif from page 36 has been pared down to leave just the outlines. You could now use this motif for a two-part stencil as on the mouse motifs on page 14.

Give texture to simple outline motifs by applying paint with different tools – a sponge creates a soft look, for example.

All in the details

Try to think laterally when deciding how to use a motif. Take the simple ladybird bug from the top of page 88, for example. Add some decorative details and it has a whole new look.

Brilliant borders

Take a motif, such as the butterfly from the top of page 85, and rotate and repeat it to create borders or frames. When joined like this the motifs create a geometrical design with a whole new look.

If one design doesn't work as a border, use two. It's fun to combine motifs and can produce a very professional look.

About turn

Sometimes you only need to make some simple adjustments to create a new look. Here, moving the head and adding two more legs to the sheep from the top of page 47 turns it sideways! Try changing antennae or eyes for the same effect.

Enhance simple motifs with goggle eyes, brads or sequins.

Techniques and mediums

Trying out different techniques and mediums is a good way of stretching your creativity, so don't limit yourself to the same materials you've always used – take the opportunity to try something new. Here's just a few to whet your appetite.

Embossing

Embossing onto foil looks impressive, creates a new look and is easy to do. Simply trace the design directly onto thick sheets of metal using an embossing tool. Place the foil over a soft surface, such as a layer of craft foam and press with the embossing tool only as hard as necessary to make your mark. For added effect paint on the foil with acrylic paint, as on the dog card, shown right.

Embossed words need to be added in reverse. Write on tracing paper then flip it over, place it on the foil and emboss the design.

Stencilling

I made two stencils from the mouse on page 37, one for the outlines and the other for the body colour. This is easier than it sounds and creates very nice results. When cutting the detailed layer, remember to leave 'bridges' of template plastic between the areas you cut out, otherwise a central area could fall away.

Decorative paper

Paper can be used in many creative ways and comes in some lovely colours and designs. It's best to start with a background sheet as a base and then stick everything else on top. Here, a pig from the top of page 48 is cut from two pink papers and stuck onto a checked background in a simple collage. I used a foam pad to attach the nose for a cute three-dimensional effect. Outliner applied around the edge of the background paper adds the finishing touch.

Packs of coordinating papers, available for scrapbooking, make this mix-and-match approach a doddle.

Fabric painting

Silk is a lovely surface to work on. Simply stretch it in a frame and slip the design underneath. You can see through the silk and trace the motif straight on top with gutta. Once the gutta is dry, paint between the lines – it's easy and fun. Here pearl gutta was used to outline the exotic bird (page 77), which was then painted in a limited palette of oranges and yellows. Sequins and foil flowers add a final flourish.

Collage

Take a motif, colour it and then colour photocopy it several times – or scan it into your computer and repeat it. Now you can cut out and stick your motifs on your cards, varnishing them for added effect. This card uses this technique with the butterfly from the bottom of page 85. Notice how it is only partially attached for a lovely three-dimensional effect.

This technique can be used on all sorts of surfaces: paper, metal or wood, and don't forget your scrapbooking pages too.

Reversing out

Reversing out is a simple but very effective technique that requires a design with a distinctive outline, such as the geese motif from page 43. For this card I traced the geese with a soft pencil onto watercolour paper. The watercolour was applied to the surrounding area only leaving the geese white. Once the paint is dried the pencil lines can be rubbed out using a soft putty rubber. Alternatively, cut your design as a mask, place it over the paper and sponge, spatter or paint on top. Remove the mask to reveal the finished effect.

Tonal images

You don't have to buy lots of expensive paints and papers to create striking images. Often you can achieve lovely results using just one colour diluted to create a range of tones. For this crab card I painted the motif from page 96 in watercolour using just one colour. For the sea-horse card on page 4, I did a similar thing on my computer, scanning in the motif and colouring it using a picture software program.

Outliners

Outliner pens are mostly used for the final embellishments, but they also work well as the main medium, creating fantastic results. These days there are lots of outliners to choose from, with many different properties, some that glitter, some with pearl or metallic finishes and some that create volume. This cuddly sheep from page 47 was drawn entirely with a gold outliner. A little colour applied to the body of the sheep provides depth.

Practice using outliner on scrap paper first until you can create an even flow.

Choosing a medium

Deciding which surface you are going to paint on is the first step in any project. Then you have to look at what paints are suitable and consider the effect you want to achieve. Crafting really does take over so make sure you set aside a clear space to work in and have plenty of time.

Metallic and pearlized paints

There are lots of fabulous metallic and pearlized paints to choose from that come as liquid paints, pens or in bottles with applicators. Some are smooth, others are lightly textured or three-dimensional. Use them to add highlights, as on this card, or even to paint an entire motif. If desired, combine these paints with foil or metallic papers for a super-shiny effect. Here a silver mat complements the metallics on the swallow and helps draw the eye in (see page 75 for this motif).

Metal leaf

Silhouetted designs, like the lion used here from page 58, are great for the modern metal leaf techniques, or you could choose a more complicated motif and simplify it until you are left with just the outline. The effect is stylish and expensive-looking, and ideal for either an entire design or a detail – what about a gold-leaf heart in one corner of a Valentine's card? Metal leaf is easy to apply. Just paint glue size over the area to be covered, then press on the thin foil and rub it down. Brush away the excess to finish. If there are any gaps, just apply more size and foil until the whole area is covered.

Save even the smallest scraps of metal leaf to use on your projects – even a tiny detail can lift a card.

Crayons, pencils and chalks

Crayons, coloured pencils and chalks are easy to use and give your work a lovely hand-drawn look. Most are available in handy sets and they will last for ages. Their soft effect is particularly useful where you want a delicate look as on this cute bear. This bear motif, from page 117, was traced onto the paper over a light box and then coloured with crayons. The flowers were scanned into a computer, printed and cut out, then attached to the card using foam pads. A colour photocopier would have done the job just as well.

Buy artist's quality pencils rather than economy versions to achieve strong, rich colours.

Watercolour and ink

When it comes to colouring a design, there's nothing to beat watercolour or ink. Watercolour can be applied in light washes, building up from pale tones to darker ones as on the cockerel card here. Inks are usually stronger in colour but can be used in the same way, allowing colours to bleed into each other for a lovely glowing effect as on this cute fox card. If desired, sharpen up an image with a little judicious pencil or pen work, perhaps to add in the fine details. These motifs are on pages 52 and 117.

Project gallery

Card making is probably the number one use for the templates in this book, but there are times when you will want to treat a friend, yourself or your home to something creative and special. Here are some ideas for using the templates for a variety of items.

Copy these designs onto flowerpots using paints suitable for outdoor use.

wonderful wellies

Turn worn wellies into works of art using acrylic paint and a few carefully chosen motifs. The green boots use the frogs from pages 104 and 105 combined with some feathery trimmings, while the yellow boots combine the glow-worm and butterfly motifs from page 85. Prime the boots first then apply your acrylic paints. You can't wear the wellies, but they make great storage containers or even plant pots.

for the birds

Craft items can be used outdoors. Here, a small wooden bird box has been primed with white gesso then painted in shades of pink. The bird motif from page 71 combines with some simple flowers to decorate the front and sides. Add a few coats of clear acrylic paint to keep your bird box looking great whatever the weather.

If you don't have a garden you could make a window box using this design.

nicely knitted

This rather lovely pale striped knitted bag displays the butterfly from page 85, demonstrating how motifs can easily be adapted for different techniques. The colours used are blues and pinks.

on the case

It's bad enough having to wear glasses, without having to put up with the horrible cases they give you. So splash out on a suede case and decorate it yourself. This design uses a pig motif from the bottom of page 48, which has been re-created in beads. Use glue to stick the beads over the traced design lines. Now your specs are a fashion item.

cute cards

Big can be beautiful, so enlarge a motif to the full size of your card. Trim around the top and right edge, making sure you leave enough card attached on the folded left edge for the card to function. This lion motif can be found on page 58 and the snail on page 86.

party pack

The tiger face design from page 59 works so well that you'll want to throw a party just so you can make these. Use the motif for party invitations, place names, cake boxes and party bags. If you are feeling adventurous, make small straw decorations or masks too. When the party is over use the design to carry over onto scrapbook pages to capture the day for all to remember. For a variation, use a monkey from page 114 or the lion from page 115.

Thomas

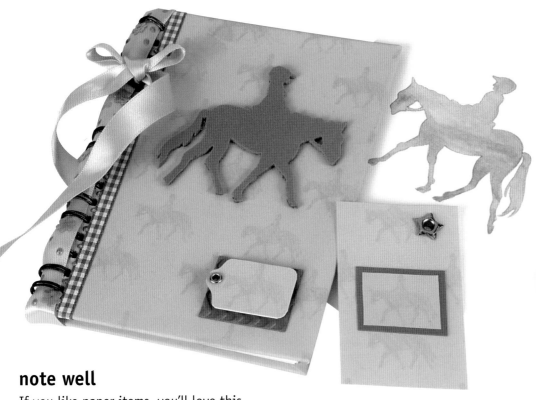

Design the cover of your notebook to hint at the contents within it.

note well

If you like paper items, you'll love this set. The background design was created by scanning the small horse motif from page 51 into a computer and repeating it until the entire area was covered. The central design is the same motif, this time cut from lilac craft foam. Add other finishing touches, such as little labels and ribbon trims. You could also paint the wire spiral with a paint-and-bake colour.

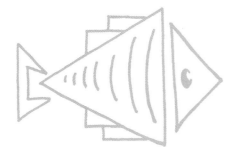

Save paper by duplicating the motif several times on one sheet of paper.

fishy fun

Make a three-dimensional card by repeating a design and layering it using sticky foam pads to raise it off the surface. Here the fish from page 40 has been drawn with a black liner onto waterolour paper with blues washed over it for a slightly faded look. If you don't want the blended effect, use a permanent marker. I scanned the coloured image onto a computer and printed it out half a dozen times so I could build up depth.

country look

Take a boring white kitchen jug and transform it with a few ceramic paints and the cockerel motif from page 44. The image was traced using the method described on page 7 then the bird was coloured with appropriate paints and the yellow background added afterwards using a stencil brush for texture. Small white dots, applied at the end, add to the country look.

If you use paint-and-bake paints you can use this idea to make a whole breakfast set.

bug's life

Jazz up your herbs and other potted plants with decorative pots. They will be a special boon in winter when flowers have faded. This pot was first given a coat of gold acrylic paint designed for outdoor use. The simple ladybird motif from page 88 was traced on top and then painted in outdoor paints too. It couldn't be easier. If your pot is to be a gift, make a matching tag using the same motif.

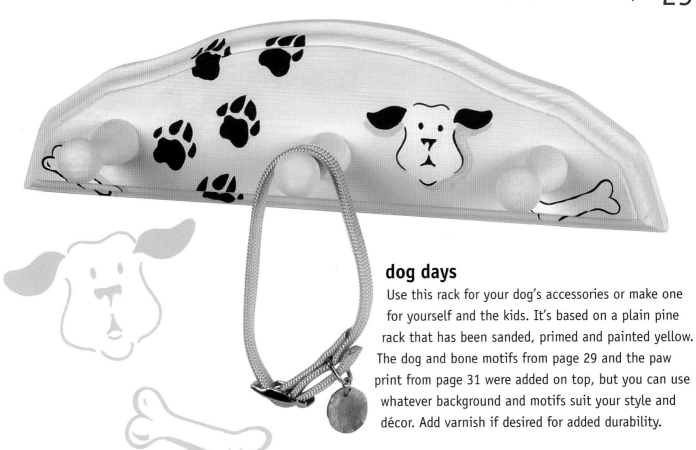

dog days

Use this rack for your dog's accessories or make one for yourself and the kids. It's based on a plain pine rack that has been sanded, primed and painted yellow. The dog and bone motifs from page 29 and the paw print from page 31 were added on top, but you can use whatever background and motifs suit your style and décor. Add varnish if desired for added durability.

tasty tin

Enamel paints are brilliant for painting tins and other metal ware and great for brightening up items that are past their best or feature designs that aren't to your taste. The motifs on this Scottie tin (see page 29) were applied with a volume outliner; the collar is a pink ribbon and has gems added to it. Tins can be primed for a flat colour or they can have the metal finish visible and use paints that allow it to show through.

Enamel paints tend to spread, making detailing difficult. Use stick-on items for these, like ribbons, gems or sequins.

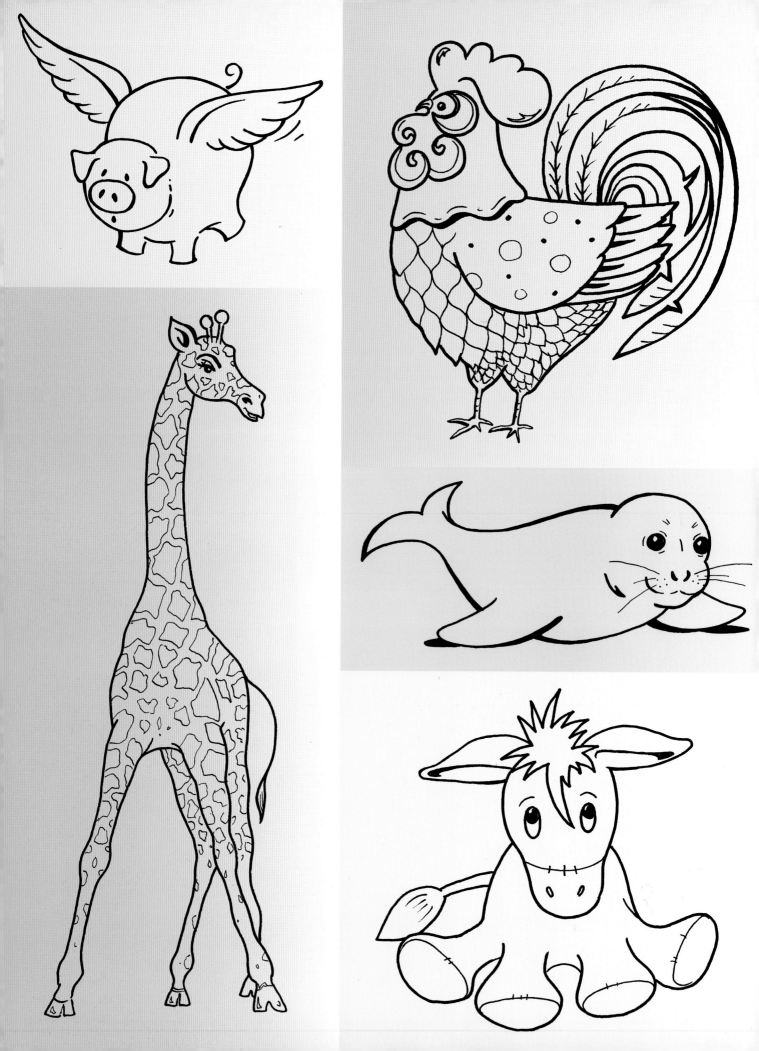

the templates

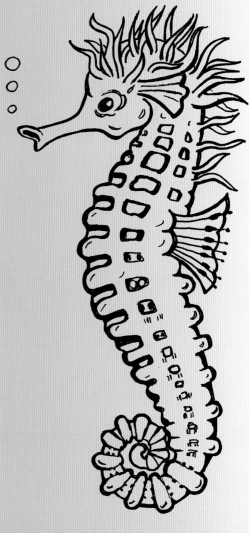

Pets' Corner

Most people in the Western world have either had a pet or would like to have one. Dogs and cats are the favourites, so this section begins with a range of these motifs (pages 29–35). There are lots to choose from, plus some useful little extras, such as a bell, bone and bowl with which to embellish your designs. And because puppies and kittens are everybody's favourites, these have their own section on pages 34–35.

Next come our other furry friends – rabbits, mice, rats and gerbils – and there's even a ferret, an increasingly popular pet. The tortoise has been placed here, as a once common house and garden pet, though it is now classed as an exotic creature and usually kept in a terrarium.

Bird lovers will find a selection of motifs on pages 38–39, including a loving pair that would be ideal on an engagement or anniversary card. Finally you'll find the fish – creatures that are popular with adults and children alike for their colourful and exotic appearances. These are ideal if you want to create a really bright, cheerful card for any age group.

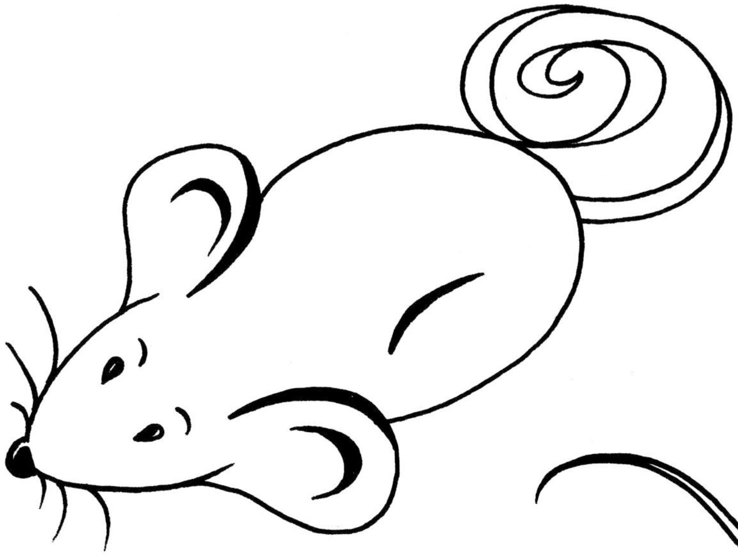

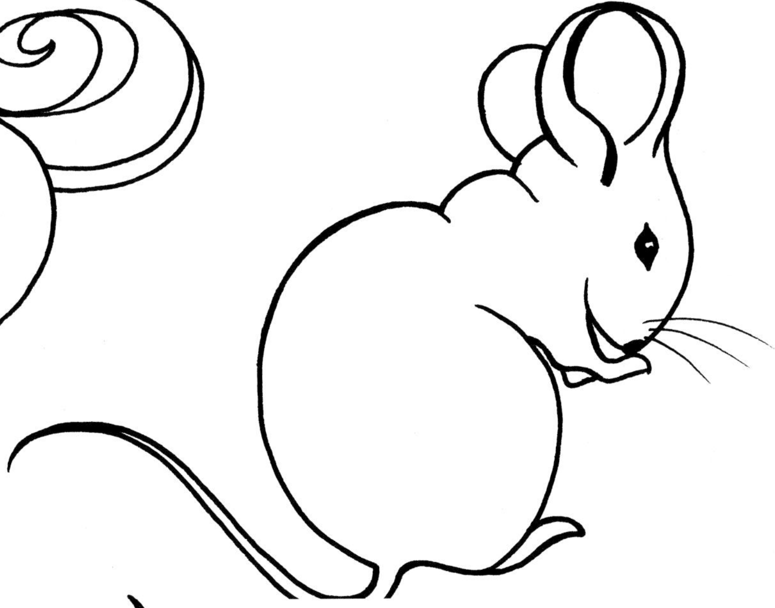

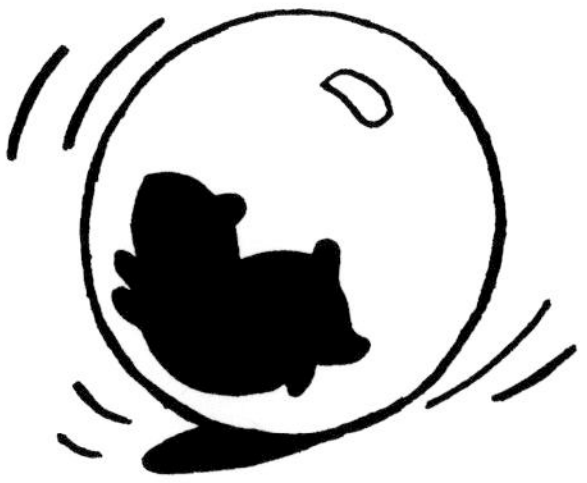

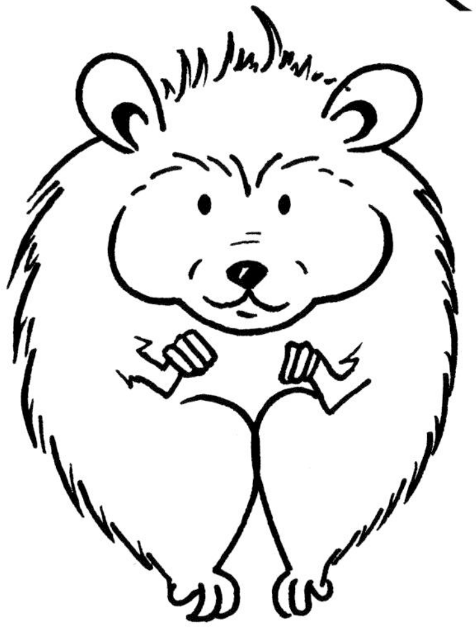

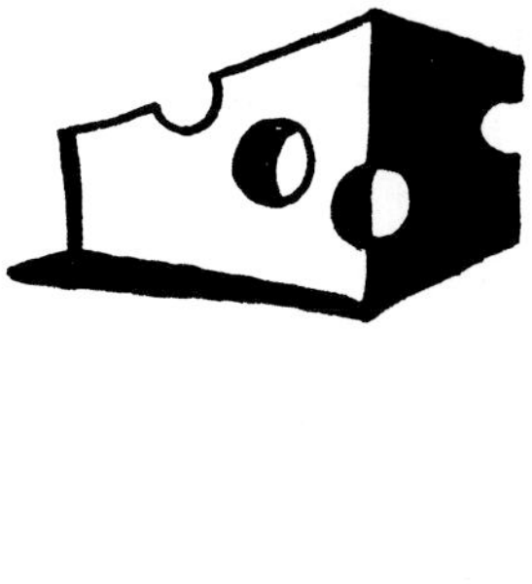

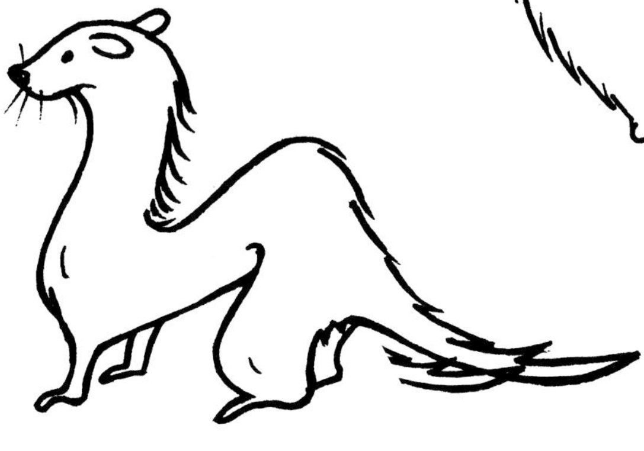

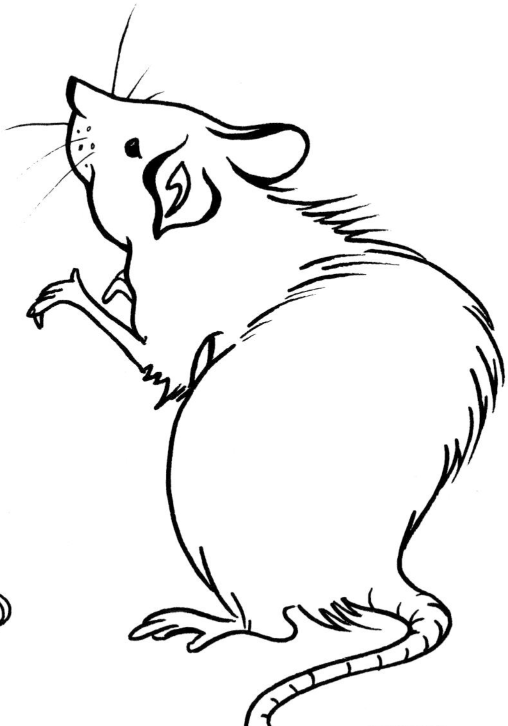

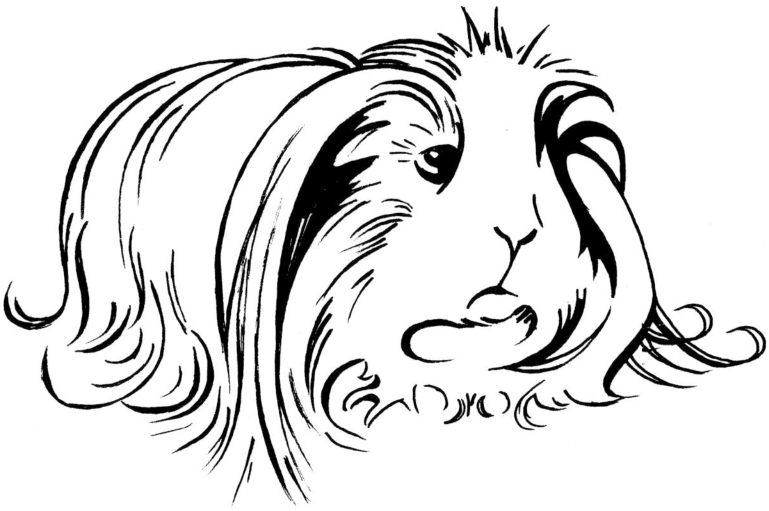

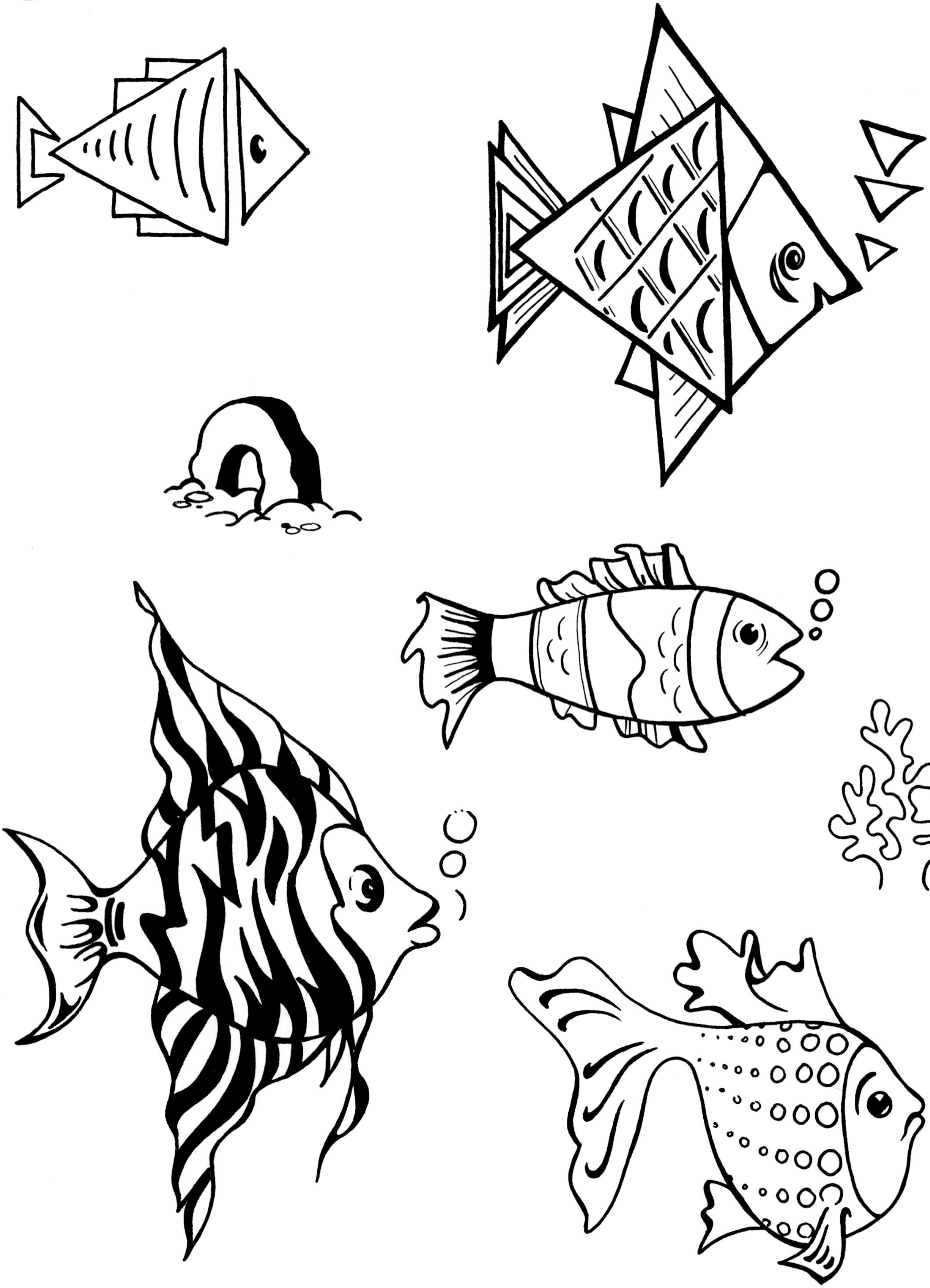

Farm and Country

From Jemima Puddle-Duck to Babe, the farm animals of fiction become familiar elements of our childhood, giving them a special place in our hearts.

This chapter starts with the birds, the ducks, turkey, roosters, hens and chicks that no picture-perfect farm would be complete without. These are ideal for general projects and especially for occasions such as Easter and Thanksgiving. Cows, sheep and goats come next (pages 46–47) followed by pigs, beloved by many for their unashamed love of food and dirt, and for their endearing shapes and expressions (pages 48–49). One of the pigs features on the card shown on page 15, and you can see the geese on page 16 and the sheep on page 17.

Ponies and donkeys are also included (pages 50–51), and no coverage of country life would be complete without the wilder side of farm life – the foxes, hares and rabbits, otters, stoats and so on that complete this chapter.

Go Wild!

Wild animals hold a fascination for us all – from the regal lions of the African reserves to polar bears living on Arctic ice floes, they are exotic, mysterious and sometimes dangerous.

You will find an amazing collection of such images in this chapter. There are lively monkeys and apes (opposite), followed by the most popular zoo animals large and small, and the sensational sights you see on safari.

The Arctic is home to an array of creatures including playful penguins, and you'll find a selection of these courageous animals on pages 64–65. Finally, travel the world to see wonderful animals from all corners of the globe from kangaroos to pandas.

For added embellishment, seek inspiration in animal furs and tracks – some examples are given on page 63.

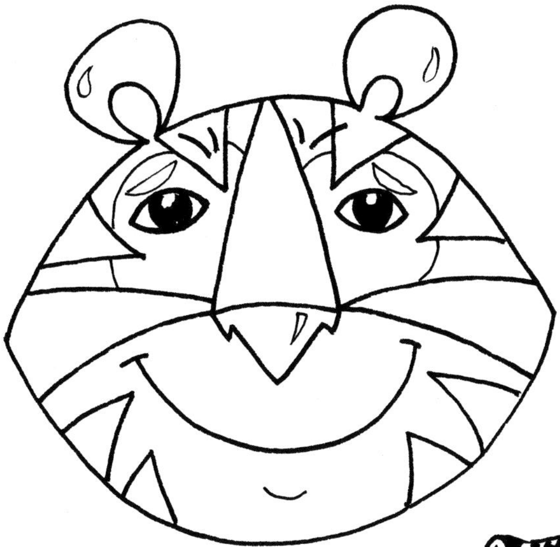

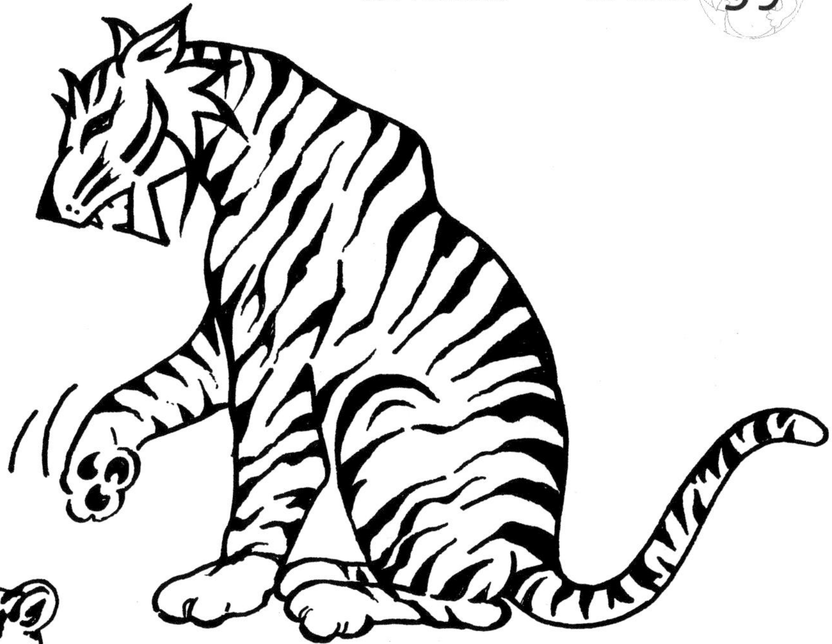

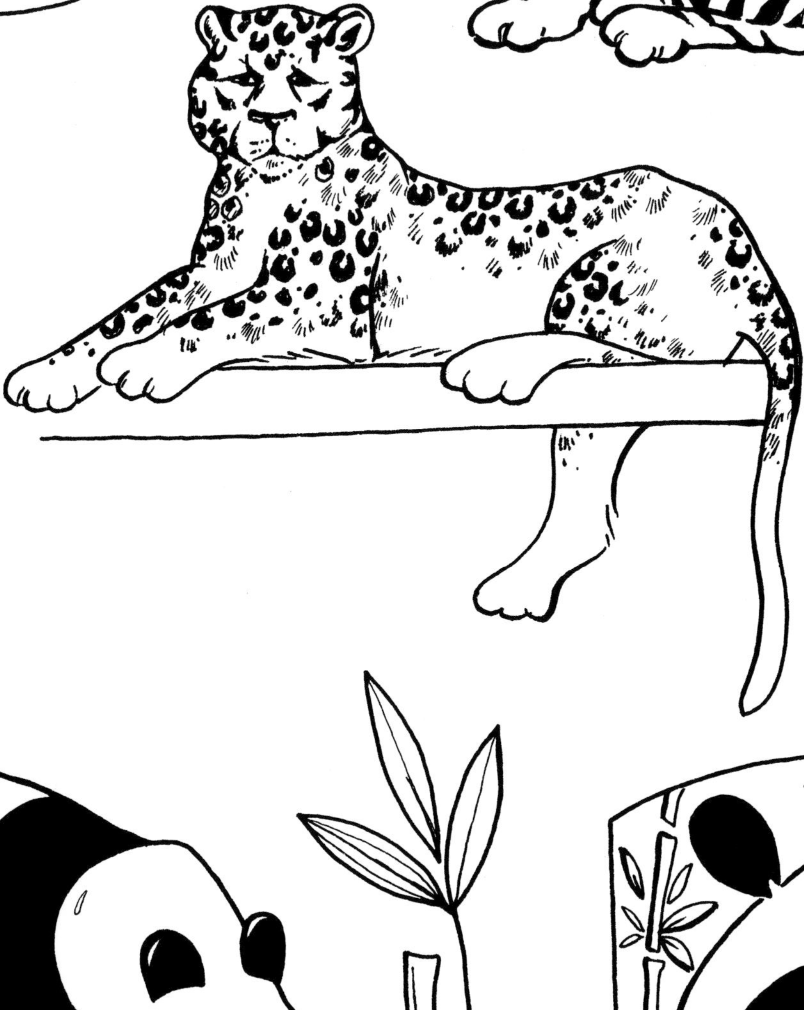

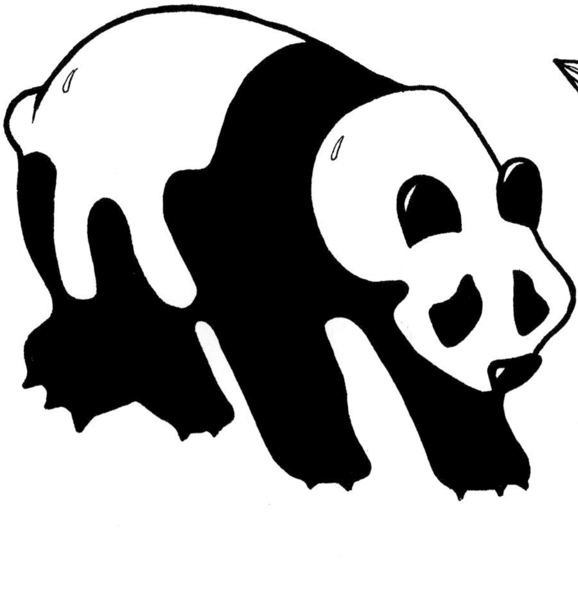

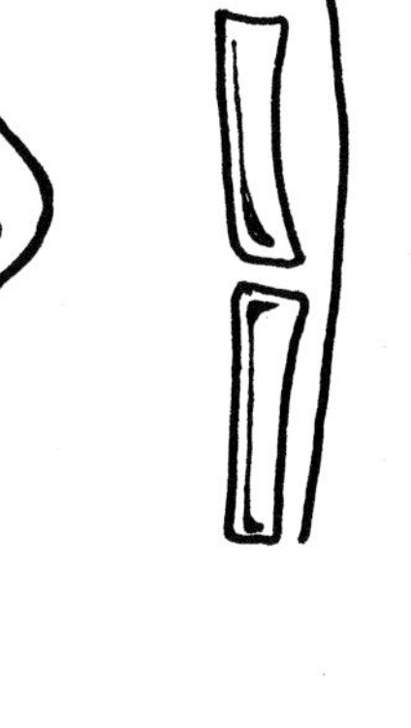

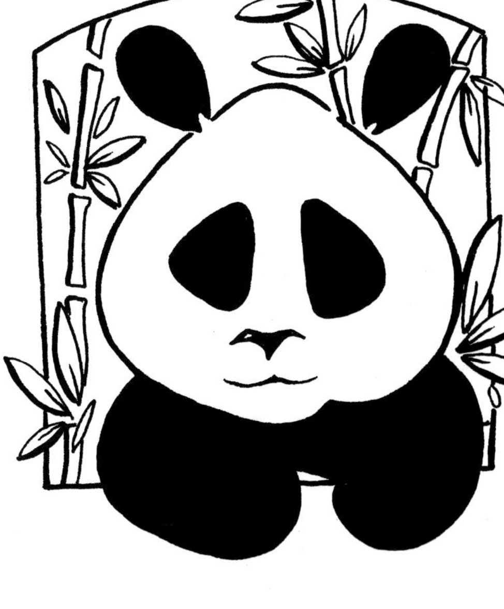

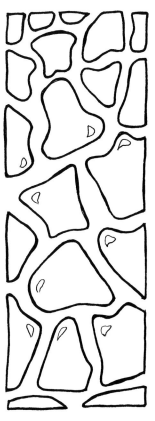

Flying High

Birds feature in crafting quite a lot, often depicted as carrying messages, as lovebirds or as the parents of a new brood. They suggest freedom and creativity, which is perhaps why we love to capture them in our artworks.

If you wish, you can use birds for their symbolic meanings: cranes for longevity and fidelity; doves for peace and love; owls for wisdom; robins for compassion and fertility; storks for children on the way, and wrens for protection against disaster.

The chapter starts with some simple images that are easily enlarged and adapted. These are followed by garden and woodland birds, and a collection designed with romance in mind (pages 76–77). The birds of prey on page 78 are perfect for marking a successful stage in a career, or to celebrate reaching an age of wisdom, while the water birds on page 79 would be ideal for wishing someone *bon voyage*. The exotic birds that end the chapter on pages 80–81 are great when you want a particularly elegant or fanciful look or as a link to far-flung places.

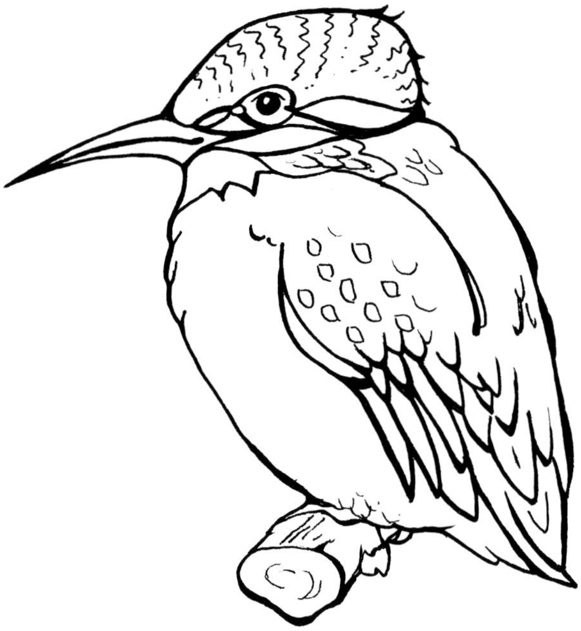

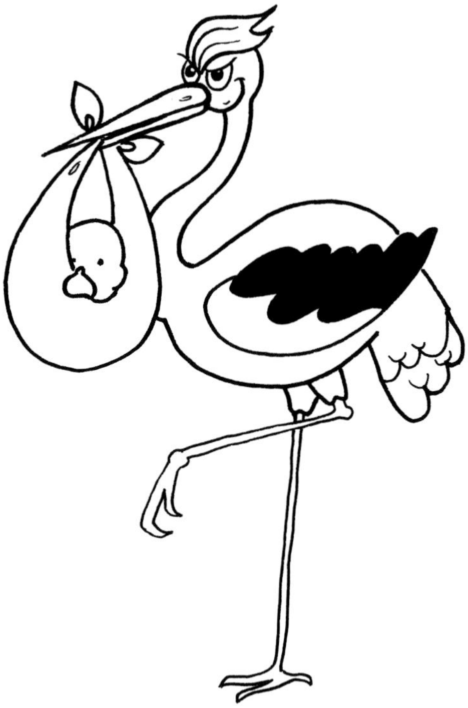

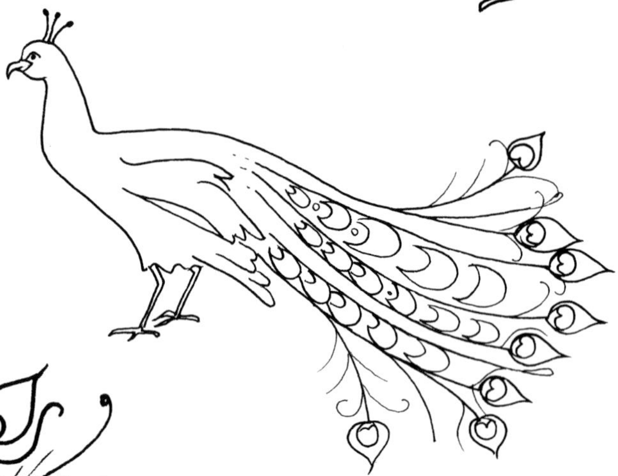

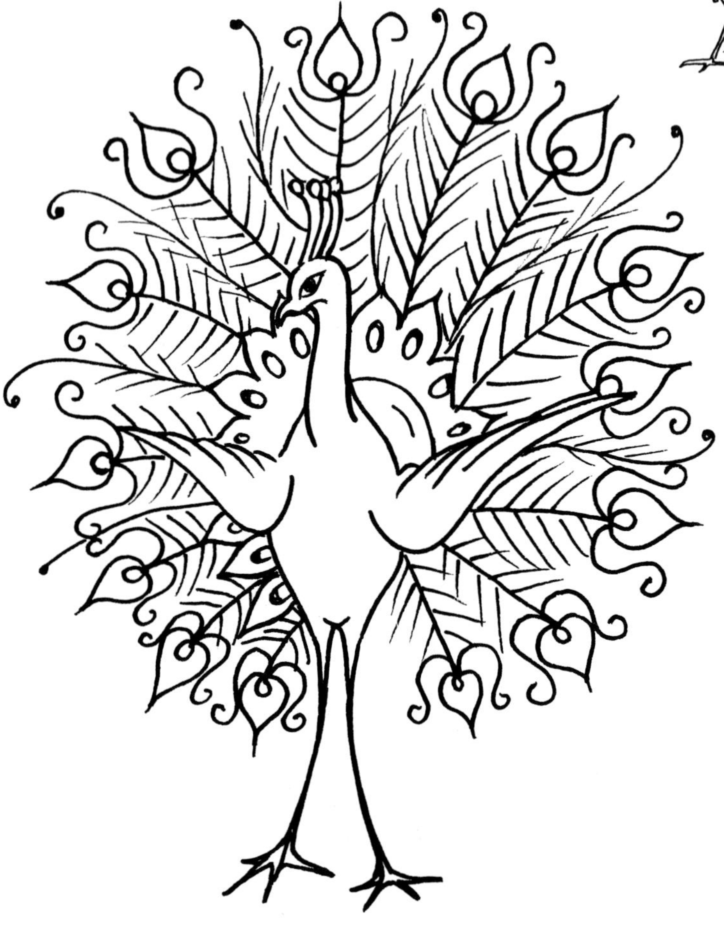

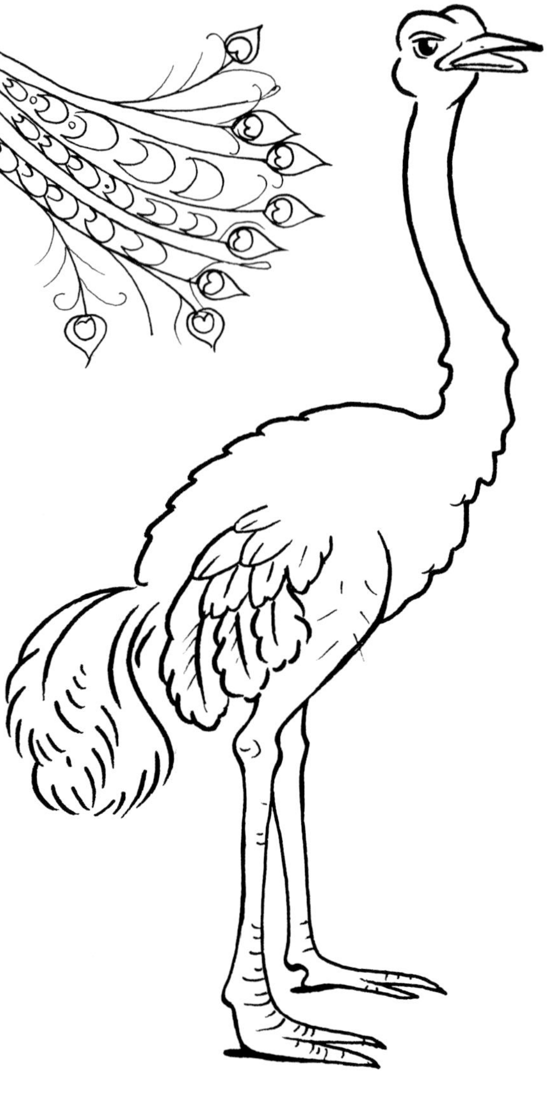

Creepy Crawlies

Despite the title, there are no horrors here, except for one or two Halloween motifs. In general this is just an interesting and useful collection of bugs that work particularly well combined with beads, outliners, iridescent powders, gems and more. Some are designed with children in mind, like the images opposite, but others have a distinctly sophisticated look.

Winged creatures feature on pages 84–85, and these work especially well as cutouts. Stick just the body down so that the wings lift off the page to suggest movement and life. For the wasps and long-legged flies, try velvet papers or thin foam for a textured look.

The snails and caterpillars on pages 86–87 can be cute to a child or horrifying to a gardener, and they've been grouped with spiders and a bat for Halloween. These are followed by ants and beetles, which make surprisingly powerful images that look simply wonderful on anything.

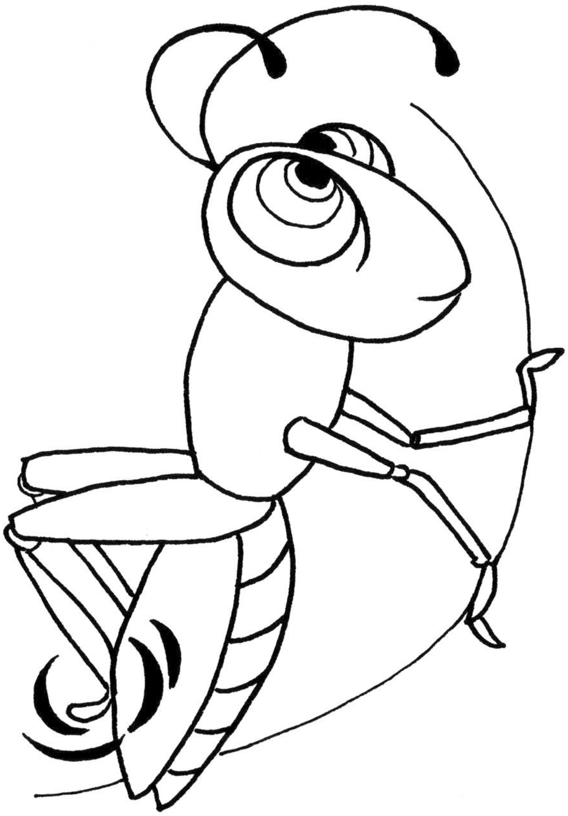

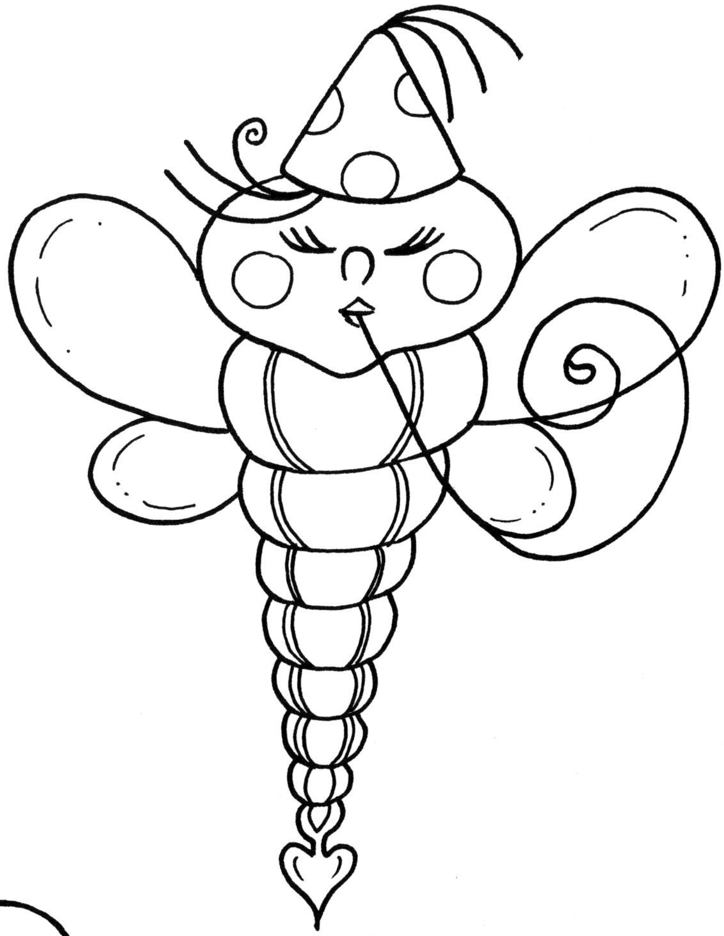

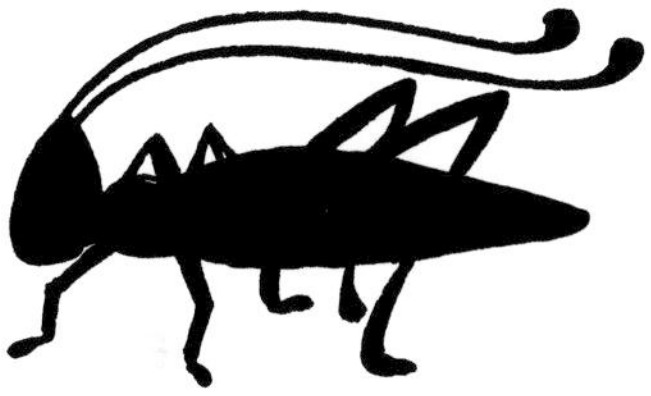

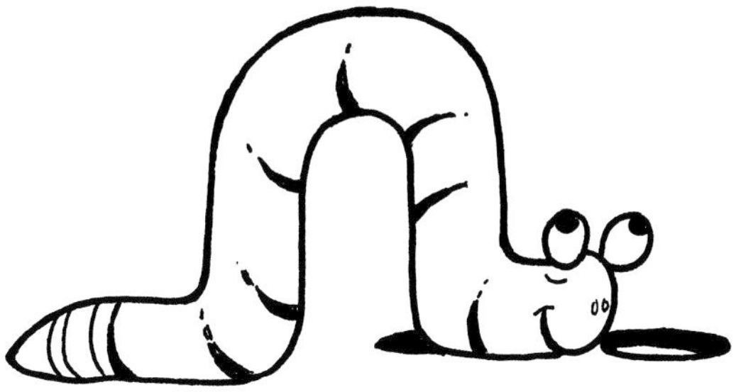

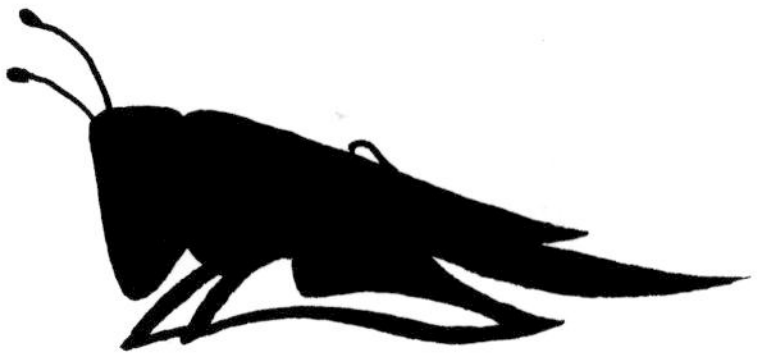

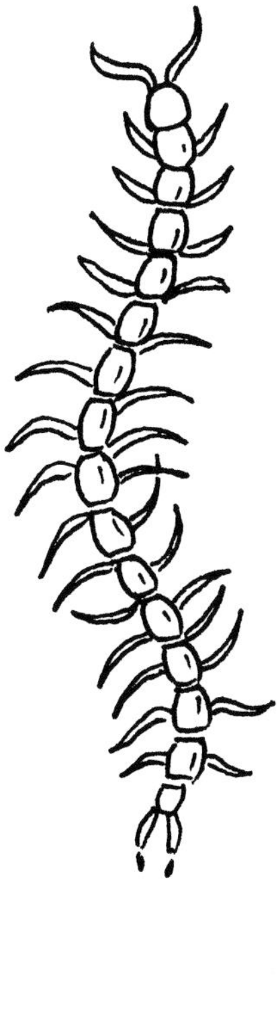

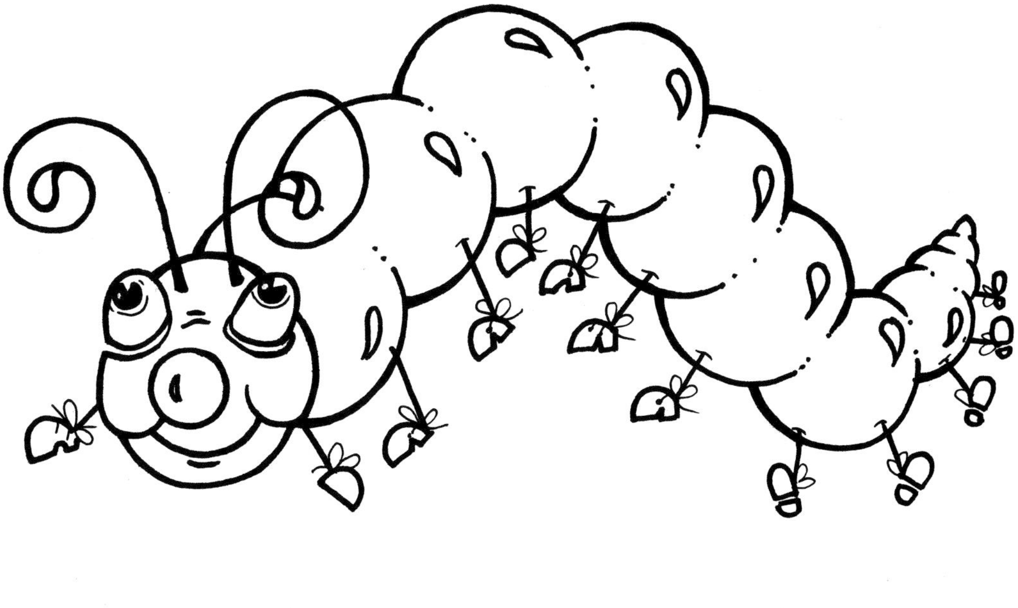

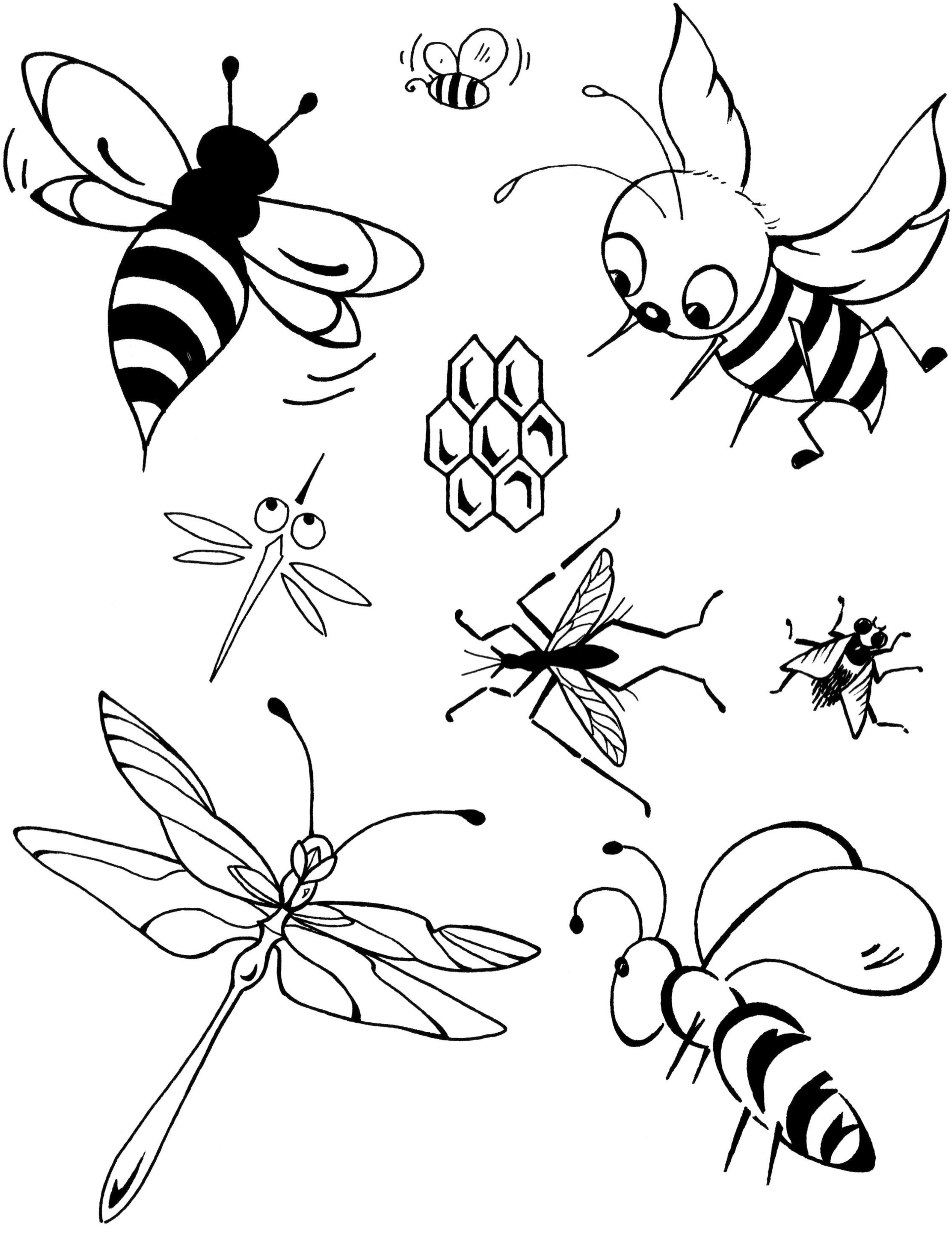

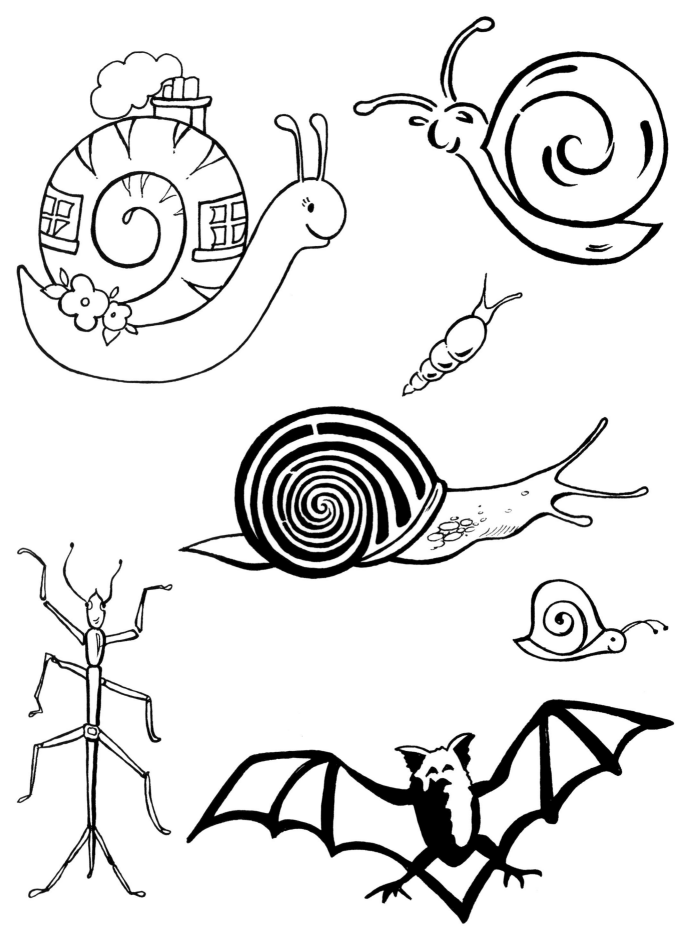

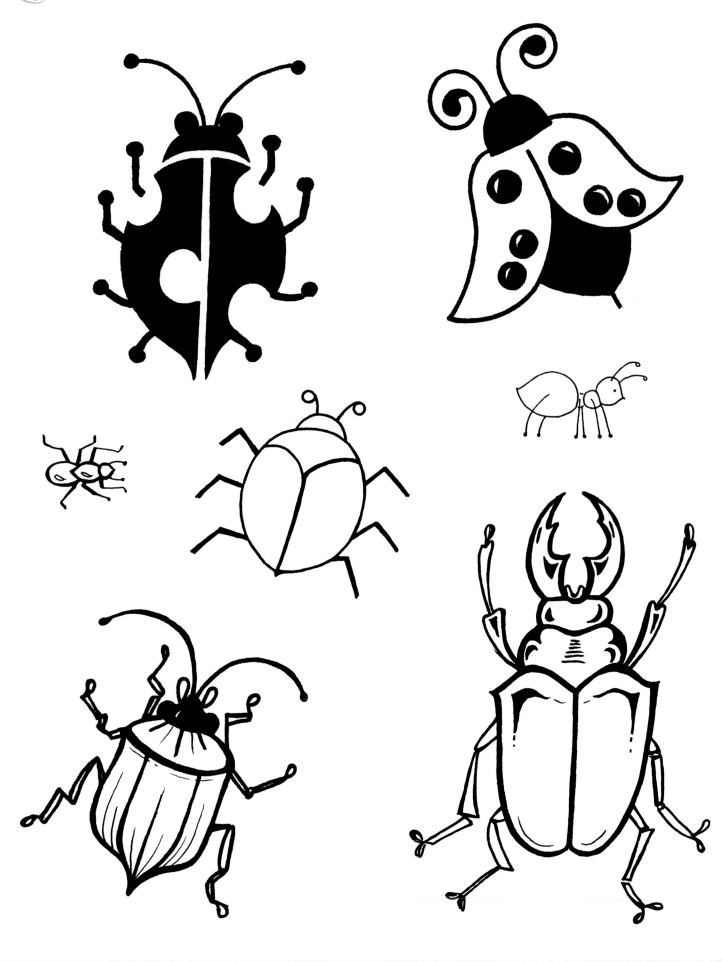

Under the Sea

From the cold, deep waters of the Arctic to the warm shallows of the Caribbean, the Earth's seas and oceans are home to some of the world's most astounding creatures. Here we can find colourful and fascinating fish, delicate sea horses, magnificent giant octopuses, eels, prawns, crabs and more. It's a whole other world, and one that holds endless fascination for children and adults alike.

This chapter begins with some basic fish motifs and then moves on to some of the more complicated fish, including the puffa, angel and dragon fish, salmon, eels and swordfish. Use them as they are, trace them in mirror image or change their size and detailing to create endless possibilities.

Page 96 is filled with crabs and shrimp, while page 97 features seahorses, starfish and jellyfish. Dolphins are on page 98, and after those, you'll find sharks, squid and octopuses – notice the octopus that is holding a banner, which is ideal for a birthday message or *bon voyage* greeting.

Slither and Jump

Not everyone's favourite creatures, reptiles such as snakes, frogs and lizards actually provide some very useable motifs. This is especially true when they are depicted humorously, as with the kissing snakes opposite, or the rather worse-for-wear party snake beside them.

Snakes can be arranged in many ways to create interesting shapes on the paper, from the simple slithering snake opposite, to the circular and swirling shapes on page 103.

Frogs and toads, featured on pages 104–105, are also very useful and easy to use – see the Wellington boots on page 20. As long as we give them cheeky grins and paint them in bright colours, perhaps with metallic touches, they make friendly, funny creatures that kids especially adore.

Lizards are very popular (pages 106–107) and have great shapes and colours, especially the chameleon, which you can colour in any way you like. These are ideal motifs for boys, tomboys and teenagers who are normally hard to please.

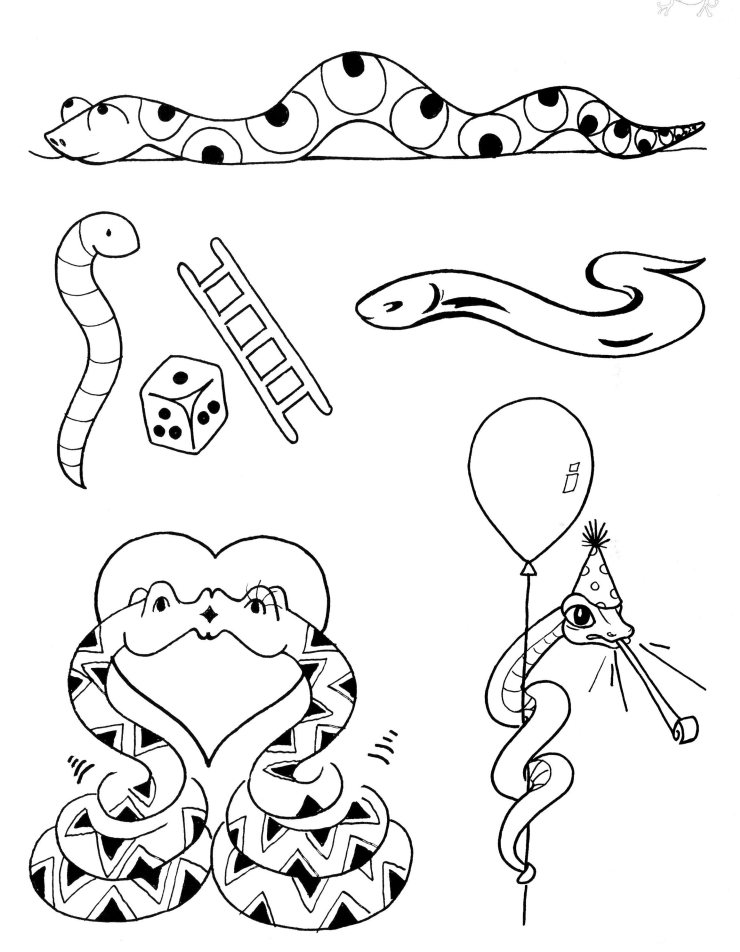

Fantasy and Fun

As children, our first introduction to many animals is filtered down through fairytales and nursery rhymes. We learn of unicorns and dragons, of black sheep, blind mice and blackbirds escaping from pies. So when catering for children it is wonderful to be able to re-create some of these images, updated in a modern style.

The chapter begins with the dinosaurs, which, though once real, are now extinct and so fit in with the mythological creatures of this section. After this are the nursery-rhyme characters – see how quickly you can identify the rhymes that go with the images on pages 110–111. You'll also find some jungle and circus animals followed by toy animals designed with a child in mind.

To conclude this book there's an animal alphabet on pages 118–119 and some borders and frames to help give your designs a wonderful finishing touch.

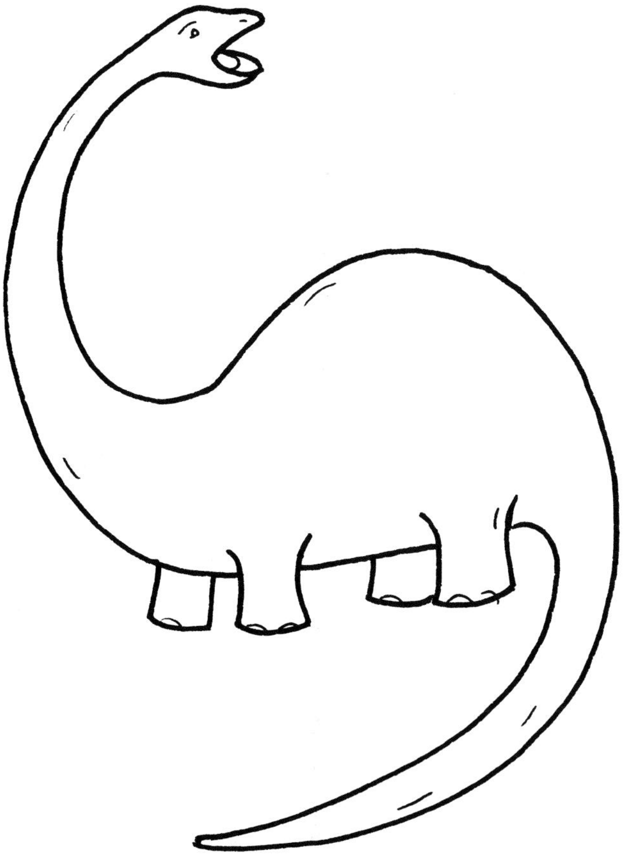

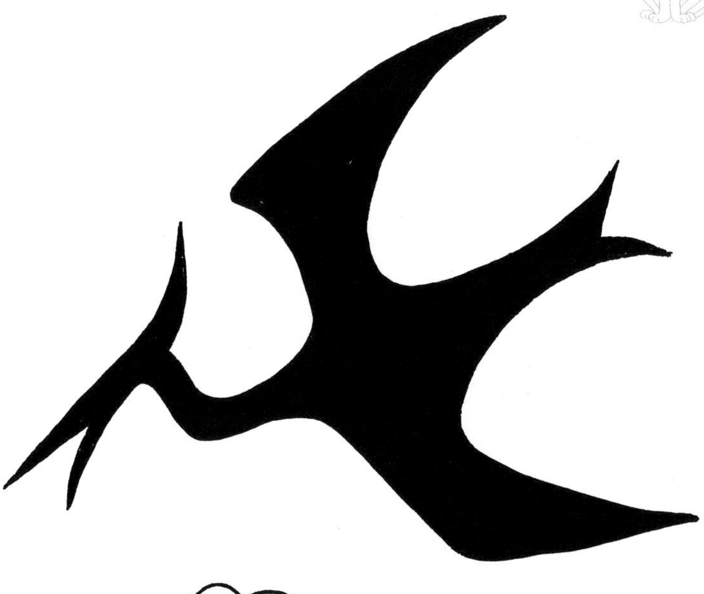

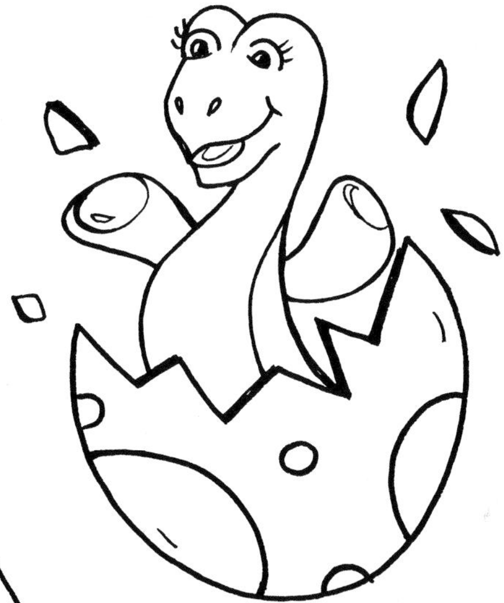

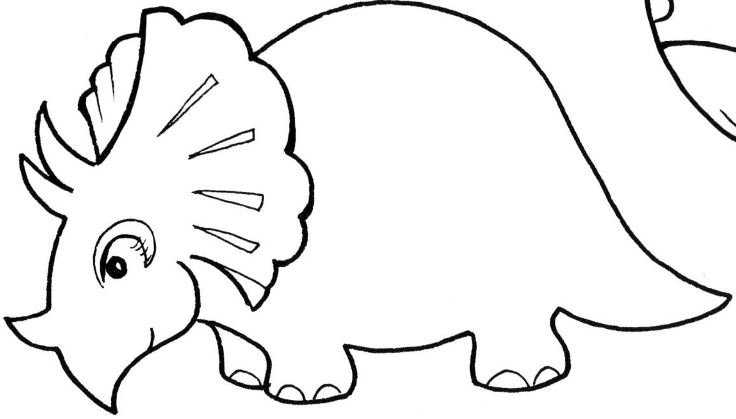

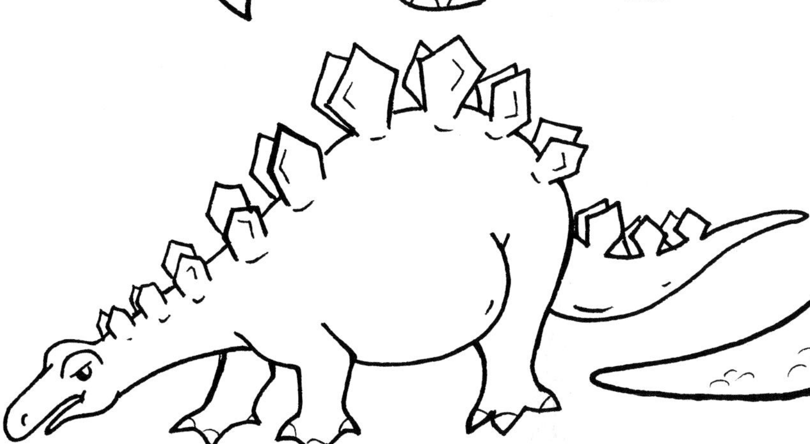

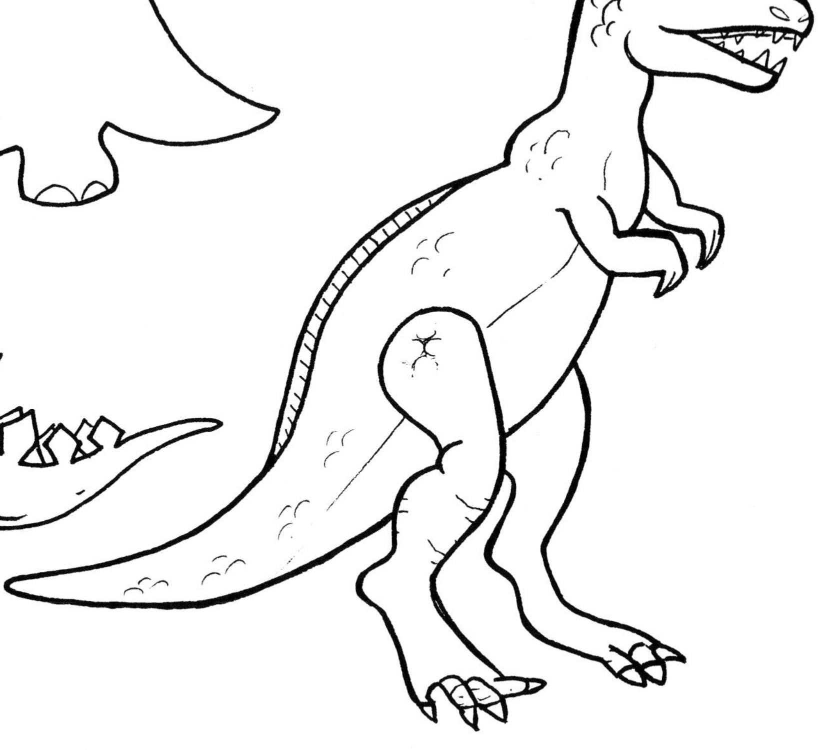

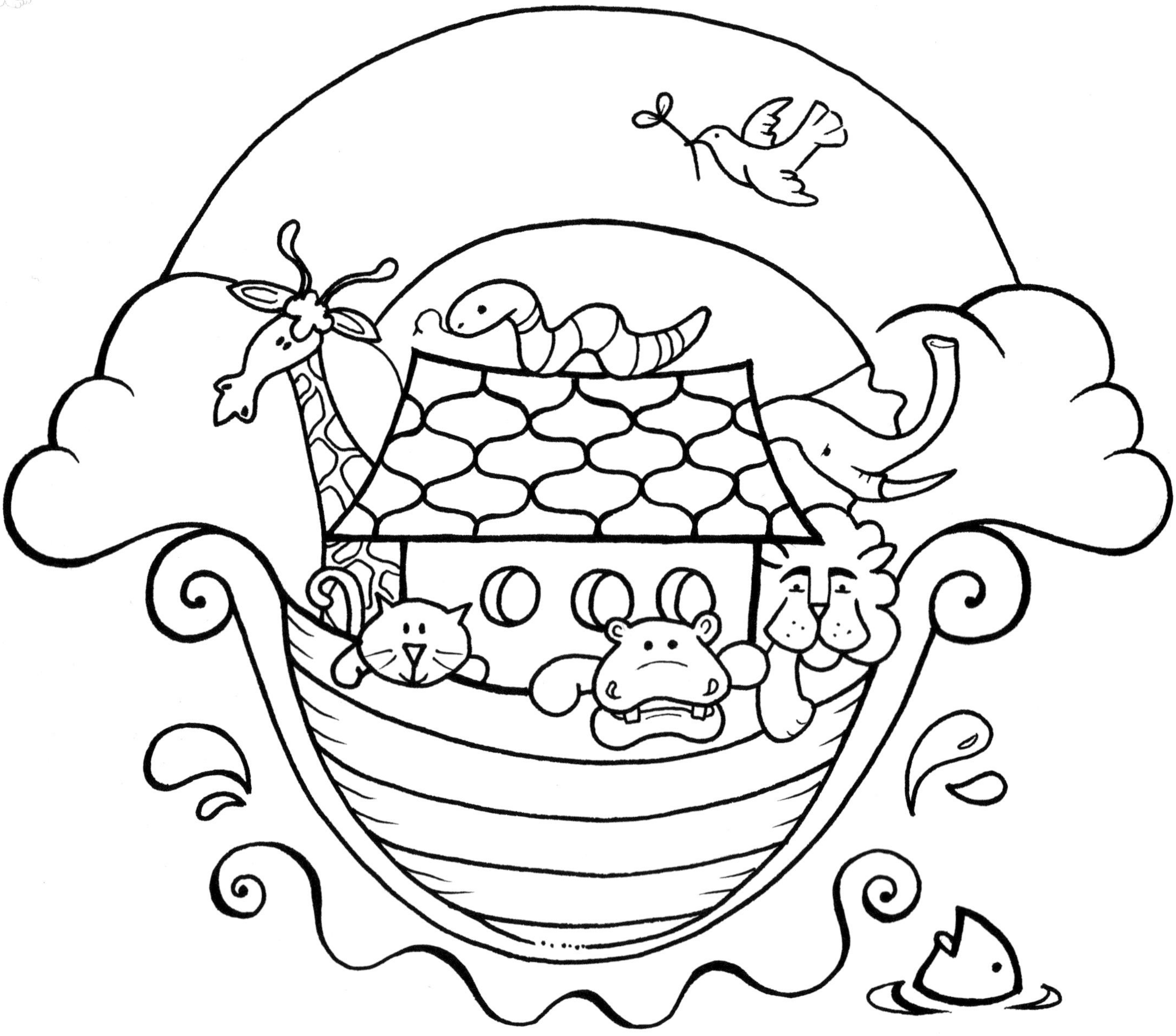

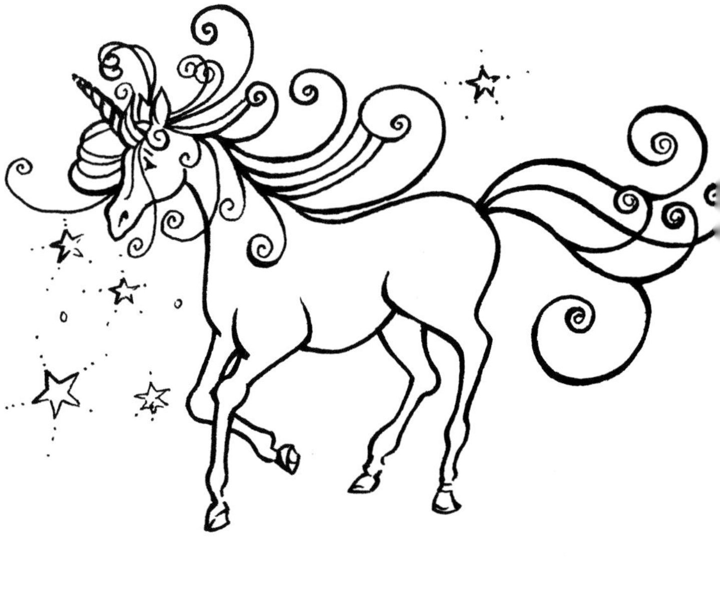

Index

About the author

Sharon Bennett studied graphics and illustration at college before embarking upon a successful career as a packaging designer for various consultancies, eventually becoming Senior Designer for a major confectionery company. In 1986 she started working on a freelance basis in order to divide her time between work and bringing up her family. It was during this time that she moved into the craft world and began to contribute projects to national UK magazines such as *Crafts Beautiful,* and worked on their craft booklets. Sharon has produced three other books in this series for David & Charles, *The Crafter's Design Library: Christmas, The Crafter's Design Library: Florals* and *The Crafter's Design Library: Celebrations.* Sharon lives with her family in Essex, UK.